P9-AGH-740

THE LEADERSHIP ACADEMY

A Conversational Approach

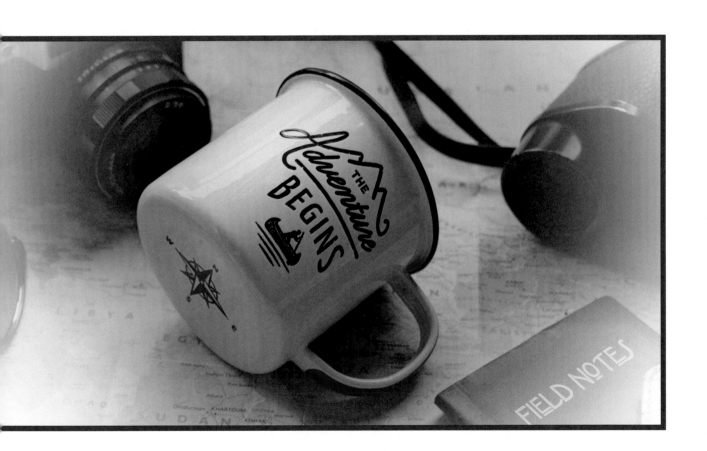

influencingO**ptions**®

THE LEADERSHIP ACADEMY

This booklet is a guide and contains practice exercises for your cohort experience of the Leadership Academy. You will have supplemental readings, videos, articles, etc., that support your learning and understanding. We will also utilize organization-specific information regarding strategy, employee engagement, performance management, diversity, equity, and functional "nuts and bolts[1]" that will begin to round out your tools for leading and managing your organization.

A CONVERSATIONAL APPROACH

Each of us is participating in many conversations at work and with our work. We can look at this concept very literally, as well as metaphorically: a conversation, by nature, is the back and forth, the listening and the sharing, the telling and the responding. When we understand and practice a conversational approach to our work, we realize that we are in relationship with individuals, teams, each other, and even ourselves. This requires paying attention, deep listening, and internal clarifying. It often takes courage because we are in conversation about things that matter to us: our work projects, our time, our livelihood, our collaborations, our frustrations, and even our lives outside of the working spaces we inhabit.

It is helpful to have some conversational tools to help us facilitate change, solve problems, and deal with things that arise. It's even better if we have tools that can help us do all of these things and create the best possible relationships. We can have positive, productive working relationships with our colleagues, supervisors, and employees—and we can reach our organizational goals and fulfill our mission and purpose. It's possible to have high performance and high trust, and our conversational nature is what helps or hinders the quality of our time at work.

THE LEADERSHIP JOURNEY

Leadership is a journey rather than a destination. Although you will have projects, programs, goals, and mileposts along the way, the terrain and weather will impact the quality of your journey with yourself, your team, and your organization. There are specific tools and skillsets that can help you become more efficient and effective. Still, it's also about the quality of the journey and the quality of your life. Having a *right relationship to livelihood* means that you are able to allow your work, your leadership, to take up the right amount of space along with your personal interests, relationships with loved ones, and participation in your community.

In this course, we will study and practice the inspirational and the practical. Every journey requires your preparation, planning, and maybe even 'getting into shape!' You can expect to examine and assess your attitudes, beliefs, expectations, and current skillsets in many areas.

The Leadership Journey

There's no linear path to this leadership journey, so we will sometimes move in direct and specific routes, and sometimes in meandering, wandering ways. Our conversations will lead us to tips and tools and often to even bigger questions, but no matter what, we will embark on the pilgrim's path together!

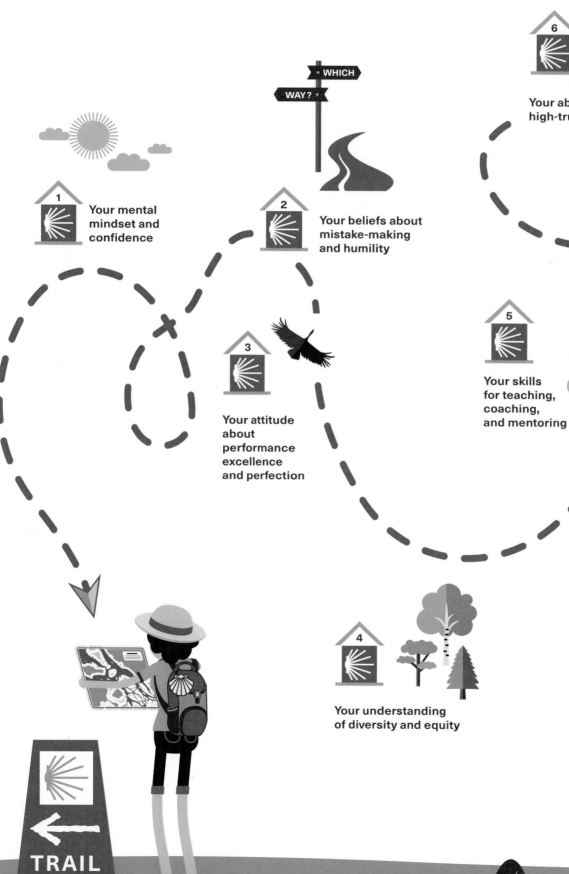

1 Your mental mindset and confidence

2 Your beliefs about mistake-making and humility

3 Your attitude about performance excellence and perfection

4 Your understanding of diversity and equity

5 Your skills for teaching, coaching, and mentoring

6 Your ability to develop high-trust relationships

WHICH WAY?

TRAIL

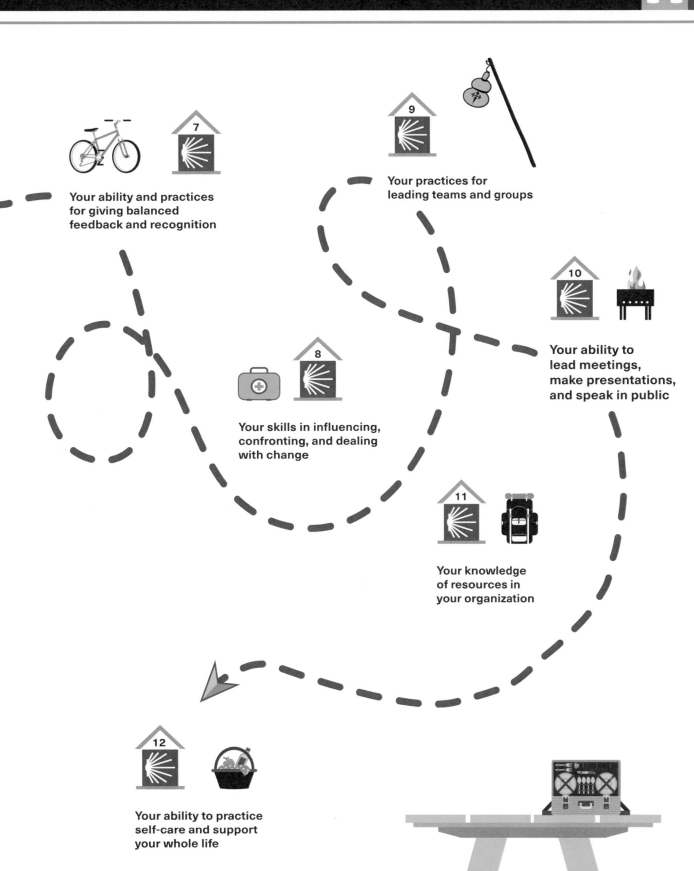

7 Your ability and practices for giving balanced feedback and recognition

9 Your practices for leading teams and groups

10 Your ability to lead meetings, make presentations, and speak in public

8 Your skills in influencing, confronting, and dealing with change

11 Your knowledge of resources in your organization

12 Your ability to practice self-care and support your whole life

LEADING IN YOUR ORGANIZATION

As a leader, manager, or supervisor in your organization, you are responsible for translating the mission, vision, and values to the people who work with and for you. You help people see where they fit and how their work impacts the big picture. It's crucial that you know and that you share the specific things important to your organization and industry. Refer to supplemental handouts or resources.

Take time to review, discuss, and jot down key ideas specific to your organization.

1. Leadership philosophy:

2. History:

3. Strategy:

4. Employee engagement or other survey indicators:

Journal Question

Considering the specifics of my organization, what's MINE to do? What specific intentions and goals do I have for my team, program or group?

YOUR MINDSET

REFLECTIONS ON *LEADERSHIP AND SELF DECEPTION*

Why begin with this book?

1. Concepts and principles are universal.

2. Growth or development begins internally.

3. A good leader must be willing to self-assess, gain clarity, recalibrate, balance, recognize gaps and inconsistencies in perception.

4. No individual or group can change without this type of honesty and humility.

Reflections and Strategies:

1. What questions come up for me?

2. Why does this matter to me?

3. How can I use this?

Pick two things you are willing to do to get and stay "*out of the box*"?

1. _____ .

2. _____ .

WHAT DOES A LEADER DO?

- Consider the following roles that may fall under the category of "leadership."

- What are the distinctions?

- What are your strengths and areas for growth?

LEADING	MANAGING	MENTORING	COACHING
Behaves strategically, holds the firmest belief, empowers, holds the vision, removes obstacles.	Ensures progress towards the goals, assigns and delegates, gets it done.	Marks the pathway and shares experience and wisdom. Listens deeply shares the story of the journey.	Sees and believes the highest potential, nudges, pushes, corrects, and praises towards it.
Reflections	Reflections	Reflections	Reflections

1. Reflecting on the chart above, place the letter "S" for "strengths" next to two of the roles you feel are your strengths and the letter G underneath the two areas you feel require growth.

2. Write the percentage of time you spend leading, managing, mentoring, and, or coaching in your current role under each of the headings above.

influencing Options®

PERFORMANCE MANAGEMENT

PERFORMANCE MANAGEMENT

In your small groups, discuss the following:

- What are the biggest challenges you face in managing performance?

- What tools do you have for managing performance on your team and in your organization?

SIX KEYS FOR MANAGING PERFORMANCE: A DIAGNOSTIC

Consider the following keys to managing performance and how they support the employee pathway. Assess each area considering both your own personal management practices and the organizational structures and resources that support them. Where are the strengths and weaknesses?

How do you feel your organization as a whole is doing with the 6 Keys?					
	KEY	DEFINITION	STRONG	AVERAGE	WEAK
			We do this well; we have clear practices and resources.	*We are 'okay' at this; some things work.*	*We have inconsistent or no solid practices.*
1.	Hire for Talent	Proactively hire the right person for the position to manage performance. Hiring processes include behavioral interviewing and assessment for cultural fit and attitude.			
2.	Set Clear, Written Performance Expectations	Positions have clearly defined expectations: specificity, criteria for good performance, and ways to measure.			
3.	Teach to Ableness	Specific on-boarding process and practices to help employees succeed. Training that allows for mistakes, feedback, skill building, and a way to measure.			
4.	Give Frequent, Small-Dose Feedback	Regular one-on-ones, balanced performance feedback, positive recognition with options for improvement.			
5.	Clear the Swamp	Regularly assess performance issues, measure consistency, and motivation, individually or as a team. Proactively identify potential obstacles.			
6.	Develop Your People	Identify multiple modalities for growth/development. Includes formal or informal mentoring leadership, skill building, and mastery of new skills.			

GAP ANALYSIS

Considering your diagnostic, identify some critical characteristics for the CURRENT state of this key element and the DESIRED state of this key element.

How do you feel your personal team is doing with the 6 Keys?				
	KEY	**DEFINITION**	**CURRENT**	**DESIRED**
1.	**Hire for Talent**	Proactively hire the right person for the position to manage performance. Hiring processes include behavioral interviewing and assessment for cultural fit and attitude.		
2.	**Set Clear, Written Performance Expectations**	Positions have clearly defined expectations: specificity, criteria for good performance, and ways to measure.		
3.	**Teach to Ableness**	Specific on-boarding process and practices to help employees succeed. Training that allows for mistakes, feedback, skill building, and a way to measure.		
4.	**Give Frequent, Small-Dose Feedback**	Regular one-on-ones, balanced performance feedback, positive recognition with options for improvement.		
5.	**Clear the Swamp**	Regularly assess performance issues, measure consistency, and motivation, individually or as a team. Proactively identify potential obstacles.		
6.	**Develop Your People**	Identify multiple modalities for growth/development. Includes formal or informal mentoring leadership, skill building, and mastery of new skills.		

Which two keys feel most important to you for your team and your attention now?

THE CONVERSATIONAL APPROACH

We are actually *in conversation* with our employees, literally and metaphorically. There are some conversations we have, whether those are in person, via phone, or video conference, or maybe text or email. All of these methods or touchpoints are ways we converse with our team members.

In the supervisor/employee relationship, there are three main types of conversations we are having:

1. The Day-to-Day conversation

A conversation to deal with emergent issues, check-in or update, ask real-time questions or resolve issues or problems. These are often ad hoc.

Suggested Frequency

These are often essential and can be challenging to manage with your own workload.

2. The Performance Conversation

A short, small-dose conversation based on a balanced approach to offering praise and recognition, as well as feedback about performance improvement or growth. These should be scheduled, planned, and periodic.

Suggested Frequency

Consistency is key here. For new performers or relationships, you might meet once per week. For consistent, high performers, once a month is often sufficient. If you have a large number of direct reports, you may need to get creative about how you connect and facilitate performance conversations.

3. The Career Conversation

This may align with an Annual Review conversation where you have time to look at someone's overall performance and goals. This is focused on long-term growth and opportunities for development, specialized training, or special projects.

Suggested Frequency

At a minimum, once per year, along with goal setting and planning. If your work and its projects change frequently, you may see opportunities for development and growth, so you can resent those in the context of your regular performance conversations.

Considering the three conversations, what percentage of your time spent one-on-one with your employee is dedicated to each?

PRINCIPLES AND PRACTICES

Performance Management is something **we do together** rather than something we do to employees. It is a two-way, focused, respectful conversation aimed at developing the employee's strengths and abilities while honoring the organization's overall goals.

The supervisor's primary role includes:

1. Ensuring that each employee is performing to standard.

2. Ensuring that the work environment supports trust, contribution, mistake-making as part of learning, and collaborative team efforts.

In essence, the supervisor is the translator of the organization's mission and vision by helping employees do their best in their jobs and creating the most conducive environment to supporting this work. We are all responsible for the technical and interpersonal aspects of our work, and the supervisor's unique role is to model, coach, support, and confront, when necessary.

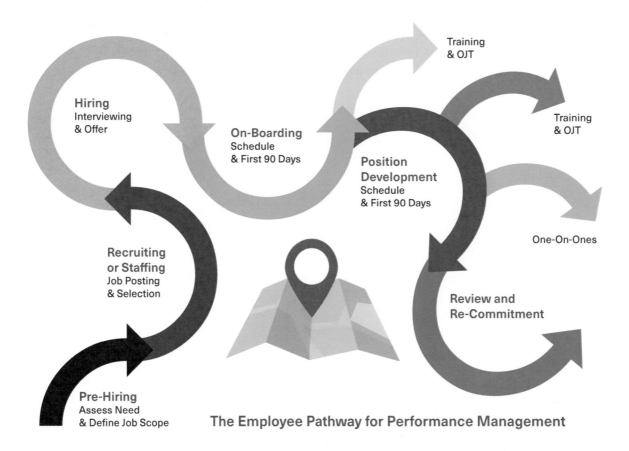

The Employee Pathway for Performance Management

Reflect and Assess

Consider **_your own hiring experience_** with this organization. Looking back, how was your employee pathway experience? On a scale of 1-3, with three being the highest, rate your experience in the space below each milestone.

Pre-Hiring	Recruiting or Staffing	Hiring	On-Boarding	Position Development	Position Development

How was your employee pathway effective?

Current State

On a scale of 1-3, with three being the highest, rate your organization and your performance as the leader of your team in the space below each milestone.

	Pre-Hiring	Recruiting or Staffing	Hiring	On-Boarding	Position Development	Position Development
The Organization						
My Team						

THE PERFORMANCE MODEL

Assessing performance and creating solutions.

Six Keys to Managing Performance

1. Hire for talent
2. Set clear expectations
3. Teach to ableness

4. Give frequent feedback
5. Clear the swamp
6. Develop young people

Managing Performance Development Levels

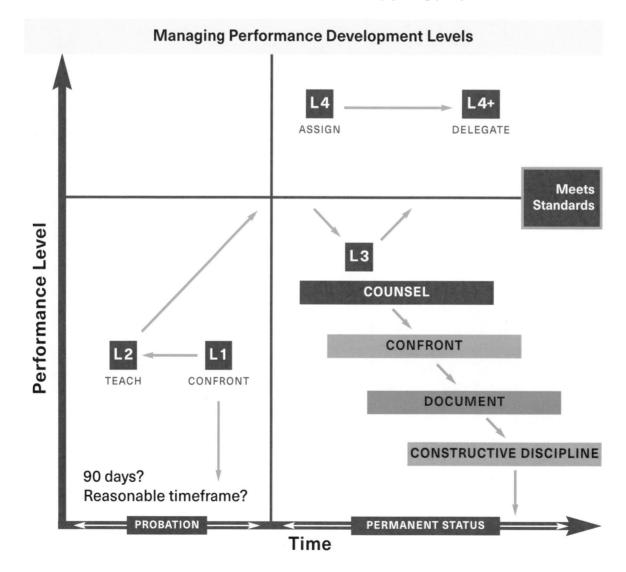

Ableness and Willingness

1. **Have you ever seen this person perform to standard, or above?**
   - **YES** → Go to question #2.
   - **NO** → Are they willing to learn?

2. **Are they performing to standard consistently?**
   - **YES** → Celebrate and recognize!
   - **NO** → Address L3.

Assessing Performance

LEVEL	ABLENESS	WILLINGNESS	YOUR PLAN
L1	No	No	Confront and communicate consequences.
L2	No	Yes	Teach, coach, and mentor.
L3	Yes	Not at the moment.	Counsel first, then confront if necessary.
L4	Yes	Yes	Assign, follow-through and sell the vision.
L4+	Yes	Yes	Delegate, ease control.

Common Profile	
LEVEL	**ABLENESS**
L1	Unable to do the task/skill, and unwilling to learn.
L2	Unable to do the task/skill, and willing to learn.
L3	Able to do the task/skill, but unwilling to perform consistently at the moment.
L4	Consistently performs to standard or above; may need to increase buy-in to team mission or vision.
L4+	Consistently performs to standard or above; trustworthy performance, star performer, can teach or lead others.

Strategies for Responding to Performance Assessment Levels		
LEVEL	**ASSESMENT**	**STRATEGIES**
L1	Unable/ Unwilling to learn	▪ Create opportunities for learning. ▪ Confront clearly and directly. ▪ State consequences of not learning and not performing to standard. ▪ Do NOT enable by prolonging probationary period, etc. ▪ Identify Timeframe.
L2	Unable/Willing to Learn	▪ Training ▪ Coaching ▪ Mentoring ▪ OJT ▪ Practice ▪ Lots of feedback
L3	Able/Unwilling (at the moment) Performance is Inconsistent and or Spotty	▪ Schedule a one-on-one to check why they arn't consistent. ▪ Ask "why" and listen. ▪ Try to identify obstacles or de-motivators. ▪ They do not need training! ▪ Clearly state expectations and timelines. ▪ If performance does not improve, move to confrontation. ▪ Document and move to discipline or corrective action (as per policy). ▪ Identify Timeframe.
L4	Able/Willing (performs to standard or above)	▪ Recognize consistent performance. ▪ Assign tasks and follow-through. ▪ Continue to create buy-in and commitment through involvement. ▪ Create opportunities for growth and development.
L4+	Able/Willing (performs to standard or above)	▪ Delegate outcome, give them responsibility for determining process. ▪ Do not micromanage. ▪ Consistently challenge and offer creative opportunities. ▪ Give them opportunities to lead and teach others. ▪ Work with them on career and long-term goals. ▪ You may not be able to retain them because they are rising stars.

SETTING CLEAR PERFORMANCE EXPECTATIONS

Clearly written performance expectations set a team member up for success and increase objectivity that we can use when we have performance conversations. Let's meet Sam, Terry, and RJ, who work for a company working on improving its performance management practices.

Video 1
The Problem with Task Lists

Key Points

Can you remember a time when a supervisor or manager wasn't specific enough? What was the result for you?

Video 2

What Do You Really Want?

Key Points

What is an example of a current task/item on your team that's not being done the way you want or to the standard you would like? Describe.

Video 3

Some of the Legal Stuff

Key Points

Where are your current strengths with providing the three primary elements: specific written expectations, training and development, feedback, and praise? Where do you need to improve?

Video 4

Nerdy Wordy Things

Key Points

Go back to your notes about Video 2. Now write a VERB + OBJECT statement and three criteria for a job well done.

Tool 10: Regular Small-Dose Feedback and Coaching

PART 1

Switch out of your leader or manager role for a moment and consider your own performance and behaviors. Think back over the past month.

1. What's an element, activity or task related to your performance of which you are happy, proud or feel a sense of accomplishment? What's good about your performance right now? Be specific.

2. What's an element, activity or task related to your performance where you need some improvement, changes or growth? How could you be better or develop?

3. When you think about what you'd like to accomplish or do in #2, what are the current obstacles, issues or problems getting in your way?

4. What sort of support do you need for #2 from your supervisor, teammates, organization, etc.? How could you be set up for success by others?

With your Conversation Partner:
Take a few moments to share the answers to questions #1-4, above. If you are listening, you can ask clarifying questions or offer affirmation. Don't try to solve a problem or give advice at this time.

PART 2

Take a look at the Small-Dose Feedback Conversation template (and put your supervisor hat back on!). If this were the template for your check-in conversation to touch base on the action plan agreed upon and shared, how might this impact the following? Discuss with your conversation partner.

1. Accountability and staying on track?

2. The overall working relationship?

Small-Dose Feedback Conversation Template / A Balanced Approach

SUPERVISOR

1. **Recognition of accomplishment or positive reinforcement of genuine attempt(s)**

    "I _____
    How you feel about what they've done.

    _____

    specifically, the way you _____

    _____
    Specific behaviors you are recognizing/reinforcing.

    and as a result, _____

    _____
    Positive impact of their behaviors.

    _____."

2. **Behavior Request: request for behavior change or request for performance improvement / development focus** (1 thing on which to focus until the next Small-Dose Feedback.)

    "I _____
    Degree of choice word or phrase.

    by that I mean, _____
    What you want.

    _____
    Specific desired behaviors.

    and as a result, _____

    _____
    Positive impact of the desired behavior, what's in it for them?

    _____."

TEAM MEMBER

3. **Obstacles to Meeting Performance Expectations**

    ASK FACILITATIVE QUESTIONS (such as):

    ☐ "What is holding you back?"

    ☐ "What do you need to do, in order to make this behavior change (or performance improvement)?"

    ☐ "What are you not ready or willing to do right now that, if you did it, would help you begin to move forward?"

4. **Support or Help Needed to Meet Expectations** (from Supervisor, Team, Company, etc.)

    ASK FACILITATIVE QUESTIONS (such as):

    ☐ "What help (or support) do you need?" From whom?

Small-Dose Feedback Conversation Results

Actions Team Member Agreed to Take	By When?	Actions Supervisor Agreed to Take	By When?

PERFORMANCE MANAGEMENT TEMPLATES AND GUIDES

A. Performance
   Expectations
   Template

B. Training and
   Development
   Template

C. Small-Dose
   Feedback Template

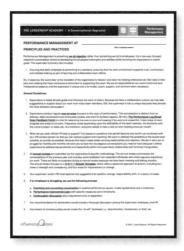

D. Page 1:
   Principles and Practices

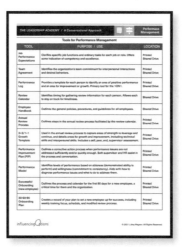

D. Page 2:
   Tools for
   Performance
   Management

E. Successful
   Onboarding Template

KEY CONCEPTS

1. We manage performance with our employees.

2. Set someone up for success with clarity and specificity.

3. The structured one-on-one is a tool for coaching and recognition. as well as course correction and prevention.

4. Assess yourself and the organization by examining the six keys.

TAKEAWAY TOOLS

Templates and Guides (See examples, left, page 24)

A. Performance Expectations Template

B. Small-Dose Feedback Template

C. Training and Development Template

D. Performance Management Overview
     Page 1: Principles and Practices
     Page 2: Tools for Performance Management

E. Successful Onboarding Template

RESOURCES

1. HR intranet site.

3. Read *The Influencing Option*, chapters 5, 6, and 7.

4. Influencing Options Videos: 1. *Trust at Work*, and 2. *Presume Good Intent.*

CONVERSATIONAL LEADERSHIP

INFLUENCING AND CONFRONTING

CONVERSATIONAL LEADERSHIP, INFLUENCING AND CONFRONTING

It isn't enough that we know our leading requires lots of conversation, but rather that we pay close attention to and adjust specific conversational or communication tools to support our goals and intentions for leadership. Often, you can consider this: you're talking to them anyway!

What if you improve the way you do it? You might have different, more effective results if you shifted how the conversation goes. Sometimes, people think that the IO way of communicating takes more time. Maybe. But mostly, it makes better use of your interactive time, creates better results, and increases performance—all while increasing trust. That's a pretty incredible return on your investment!

■   Who is someone you need to influence now with regards to their performance?

A CONVERSATION PLANNER

It helps to take some time to assess or diagnose an important conversation that you want to have or that you've tried to have to see how you might shift or change your approach. The Conversation Planner tool invites you to assess the following:

- Assess the relationship and conversation foundation.
- Assess my thinking.
- Assess trust and current conversation.

Let's take a look at a current important conversation that you either are having or need to have:

PART 1 / ASSESS THE RELATIONSHIP AND CONVERSATION FOUNDATION

☐ Commitment to a shared vision (you're on the same page)?

☐ Relationship based on earned trust (you have personal power)?

How do you know?

PART 2 / ASSESS MY THINKING ⇄ What is the story I'm telling myself?

☐ Presuming negative intent (your interaction is "in the box" with limited possibilities)?

☐ Presuming good/positive intent (your interaction is "out of the box" with unlimited possibilities)?

How do you know?

Am I balancing honesty, accountability and respect?

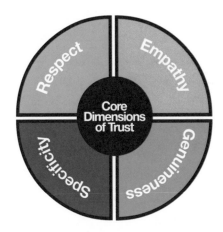

☐ Emphasizing accountability with brutal honesty?

☐ Emphasizing respect with partial honesty?

☐ Conversation has balanced accountability and respect: are you telling the truth in a way that preserves the relationship by keeping their defensiveness low and trust high, so they can hear and receive it?

PART 3 / ASSESS TRUST AND CURRENT CONVERSATION

Am I communicating with high levels of the Core Dimensions? Is my current conversation balanced?

↻ Respect

- Sharing the "why" behind the "what"?
- Soliciting their feedback or concerns?
- Listening to feedback or concerns?
- Patiently supporting the learning and change process?

Which of these do I need to improve?

1. _____

2. _____

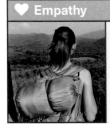

♥ Empathy

- Asking clarifying questions to understand why they feel/think the way they do?
- Verbally acknowledging their current feelings/opinions about the change?
- Behaviorally demonstrating acceptance for what they feel/think and why.
- Normalizing feelings; making it okay to be temporarily resistant, worried, cautious, etc.?

Which of these do I need to improve?

1. _____

2. _____

Genuineness

- Being transparent about your feelings, opinions or concerns?
- Keeping promises: following up and following through?
- Owning your own mistakes, misunderstandings or missteps?
- Being upfront about your role to hold them accountable to these expectations?

Which of these do I need to improve?

1. _____

2. _____

Specificity

- Being very clear about expectations, including timeframes and due dates?
- Providing detailed and relevant descriptions or models for what success looks like?
- Checking for understanding of expectations and time frames; asking what can I clarify?
- Using specificity in reverse: asking/helping to address specific issues, obstacles.

Which of these do I need to improve?

1. _____

2. _____

Notes from my partner exercise:

_____

_____

_____

_____

PREPARE TO INFLUENCE WITH A BEHAVIOR REQUEST

Video 1
Influencing and Confronting

Key Points
What are some things that are important to do within an employee's first 90 days? What might be the reason Cherise hasn't asked for help?

Video 2

The Influencing Request Prep Tool

Key Points

Why might you take such a close look at preparing for an influencing conversation? When would this not be necessary?

Video 3

The Behavior Request

Key Points

List three positive outcomes of the conversation with Cherise and Sam. 2. What might happen if Sam's request is short and sweet—"Cherise, I need you to increase your productivity"?

The Behavior Request

Write a direct and respectful Behavior Request, using the template, below. Remember to check again for Specificity!

> "I _____ (Circle one)   wonder if you could   would like you to consider   would like you to   prefer   want   need   expect   demand _____
>
> Word or phrase indicating degree of choice you're giving, i.e. how acceptable it would be to give you a "no", progressing from low to high control.
>
> _____
> What you want.
>
> by that I mean, _____
> Specificity: specific desired behaviors.
>
> _____
>
> and as a result, _____
> Positive Natural Consequences: positive impact, why it's important to you, answer the WIIFM question - what's in it for them?
>
> _____."

Video 4
Confronting with Respect

Key Points

How should Sam handle this? Should she have said something during the meeting? What's wrong with Tyler's attitude?

The Confrontation Continuum

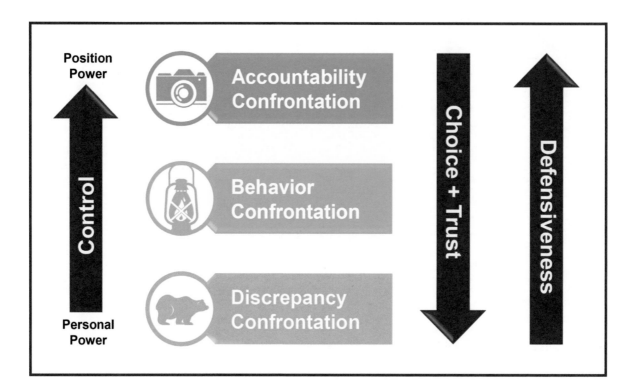

Control

_____

_____

Choice and Trust

_____

_____

Defensiveness

_____

_____

Video 5
The Discrepancy Confrontation

Key Points
What might have happened if Sam had jumped right into a Behavior Request Confrontation with Tyler? When would you skip the Discrepancy Confrontation?

The Discrepancy Confrontation

"I'm (circle one) _____ confused   concerned   frustrated _____ because on the one hand
_____
Feeling word.

_____ while on the other hand
Past positive behavior or agreement.

_____."
Specific example of mismatched behavior.

THE BEHAVIOR REQUEST AS A CONFRONTATION

A basic behavior request, or influencing request, is the same as a behavior request delivered as a confrontation, except for context. Here you address what you need directly and respectfully, with the clarity you need to provide about what you want instead of what's currently happening.

Two things can help with confrontations:

Converting undesirable to desirable—helps you ask for what you want instead of what you don't want.
Framing your conversation helps the other person understand your intention, goal, or point of view.

> "I _____ (Circle one)   wonder if you could   would like you to consider   would like you to   prefer   want   need   expect   demand
> Word or phrase indicating degree of choice you're giving, i.e. how acceptable it would be
> to give you a "no", progressing from low to high control.
>
> _____
> What you want.
>
> by that I mean, _____
> Specificity: specific desired behaviors.
>
> _____
>
> and as a result, _____
> Positive Natural Consequences: positive impact, why it's important to you,
> answer the WIIFM question - what's in it for them?
>
> _____ ."

Last Resort, The Accountability Confrontation

Used rarely and only when you've tried everything else. After the person's response, you will need to take action.

> "Are you willing to _____ , yes or no?"
> What you want or have requested.

- If "<u>yes</u>," move to specificity, and especially the timeframe.

- If "<u>no</u>," identify and share consequences: a written warning, PIP, reassignment, or termination.

KEY CONCEPTS

1. Assess your foundations for influencing.

2. Influencing with integrity means we get what we want or need while also increasing trust.

3. We use the Influencing Options concepts as the foundation for influencing and confronting.

4. Confronting = respectfully resolving an issue.

5. Position power is a most useful tool in an emergency/crisis or last resort.

TAKEAWAY TOOLS

Templates and Guides

A. The **Conversation Planner**

B. Influencing Drafting Tool

C. Confrontation Drafting Tool

RESOURCES

1. HR intranet site.

3. Read *The Influencing Option*, chapters 6, and 7.

4. Influencing Options Videos: 1. *Telling the Truth*, and 2. *Trust at Work*.

A. Conversation Planner

B. Influencing Drafting Tool

C. Confrontation Drafting Tool

THE CHANGE JOURNEY

STAGE 1 EMOTIONAL ZONE	STAGE 2 REFLECTION ZONE		STAGE 3 COMMITMENT ZONE
REACTING EMOTIONALLY →	ACCEPTING RESPONSIBILITY →	EVALUATING AND DECIDING →	TAKING ACTION
■ Externalizing: blaming	■ Personalizing: "I" messages	■ Brainstorming	■ Planning and carrying out the action(s) they can live with
■ Venting/out loud or internal	■ May be out loud or internal	■ Weighing pros and cons of options	■ Demonstrating behavioral commitment
■ Smoke-screening: avoiding problem solving	■ Reflecting	■ Considering the risks, costs and benefits	■ Experimenting, discovery and learning
■ Distressful/only temporary relief	■ Letting go	■ Deciding what they can live with	■ Integrating the change into their new normal
■ Potentially toxic to self and others	■ Conscious effort to problem Solve and/or change		
	■ Does not distress others		
	■ Creates hope		
	■ Demonstrates empowerment		

THEM

YOU

Performance

Time

THE CHANGE JOURNEY / An Ongoing Conversation

influencing Options®

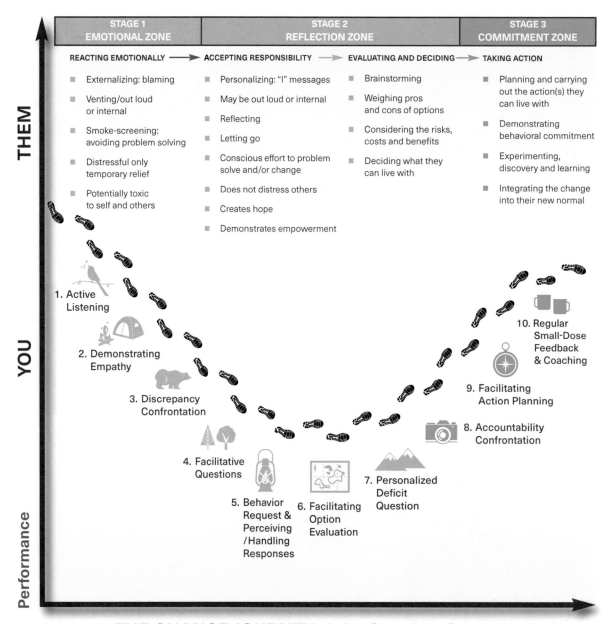

STAGE 1 EMOTIONAL ZONE	STAGE 2 REFLECTION ZONE		STAGE 3 COMMITMENT ZONE
REACTING EMOTIONALLY →	ACCEPTING RESPONSIBILITY →	EVALUATING AND DECIDING →	TAKING ACTION
■ Externalizing: blaming	■ Personalizing: "I" messages	■ Brainstorming	■ Planning and carrying out the action(s) they can live with
■ Venting/out loud or internal	■ May be out loud or internal	■ Weighing pros and cons of options	■ Demonstrating behavioral commitment
■ Smoke-screening: avoiding problem solving	■ Reflecting	■ Considering the risks, costs and benefits	■ Experimenting, discovery and learning
■ Distressful only temporary relief	■ Letting go	■ Deciding what they can live with	■ Integrating the change into their new normal
■ Potentially toxic to self and others	■ Conscious effort to problem solve and/or change		
	■ Does not distress others		
	■ Creates hope		
	■ Demonstrates empowerment		

THEM

YOU

Performance

1. Active Listening

2. Demonstrating Empathy

3. Discrepancy Confrontation

4. Facilitative Questions

5. Behavior Request & Perceiving /Handling Responses

6. Facilitating Option Evaluation

7. Personalized Deficit Question

8. Accountability Confrontation

9. Facilitating Action Planning

10. Regular Small-Dose Feedback & Coaching

Time   **THE CHANGE JOURNEY / An Ongoing Conversation**

As you listen and discuss the Change Journey and the Ten Tools, mark the following on the model:

■ Areas of Strength (mark with an S).

■ Areas for Growth (mark with a G).

Ten Conversational Tools for Facilitating Change

	TOOL	KEY DEFINITION	WHEN TO USE
1	Active Listening	Listening with intent to understand the content of what is shared. Using clarifying questions and summarizing statements in conversation. Ongoing conversational tool.	When you are trying to understand the context of a situation; when you are unclear about what's going on; when the other person feels you don't understand them.
2	Demonstrating Empathy	Showing that you understand what someone is feeling, why they feel that way, without judgment. One of the Core Dimensions for Trust. Ongoing conversational tool.	When there is a lot of emotional content in a situation; when you need to understand how someone is feeling in order to deescalate high emotion; when the other person needs to feel heard and seen by you.
3	Discrepancy Confrontation	A low-risk confrontation that points out a mismatch or lack of congruence between what is currently happening and what was either past positive behavior or an agreed-upon behavior.	When you are confused by the mismatch; when you want to open a conversation with openness and curiosity; when you want to express concern or frustration in a respectful way.
4	Facilitative Questions	Questions to help gain clarity and to help someone move through the process of problem-solving or gaining understanding. Generally open-ended and future-focused. Ongoing conversational tool.	When you are engaged in Active Listening and you are balancing your communication; when you want to help someone get unstuck and out of their 'story' to move forward; when you need to move beyond 'why' questions.
5	Behavior Request and Perceiving/ Handling Responses	A direct, specific and respectful request for a behavioral commitment and change. Utilizes all the Core Dimensions. A Recognition of how someone says 'no' and potential 'smoke screens' and how to respond to them.	When you feel you understand the context and you need to communicate your desire for action and behavior change; when you need to be clear about what you want; when you listen for and receive a response to your request.
6	Facilitating Option Evaluation (The Three Empowered Choices)	A model for understanding the three empowered choices we have for responding to something that's causing us distress: Influence, Acceptance and Removal. An understanding of the Toxic Zone, its risks and indicators, and how to help someone get out of Victim Mode.	When someone sounds stuck in a negative or ineffective story; when you need someone to 'move on' and get out of the Toxic Zone; when you are helping someone evaluate the options that are best for them to deal with a situation.
7	Personalized Deficit Question	A question that asks to suspend all of the reasons why a change cannot occur and engages them in identifying the 'real' problem for them in moving forward.	When you identify that someone needs help identifying the 'real' issue and their reluctance to deal with it; when you are supporting someone taking action that will move them toward solution or resolution.
8	Accountability Confrontation	A direct confrontation that asks a yes/no question. High risk for defensiveness and can be perceived as confrontational. Useful to gain a quick answer of commitment. Can be a use of position power, depending on the context.	When you feel you are at a turning point or 'last resort' in the conversation and need to have clarification about someone's willingness; when you are also willing to take action, depending on the answer; when you have tried all other forms of influencing.
9	Facilitating Action Planning	A conversation to clarify the Who, What, Where, When, Why and How of the person's plan. A collaborative or reflective process to gain a specific behavioral commitment to the change.	When the person has moved through the Reflection Zone in the Change Journey and is ready to behaviorally commit to action; when anticipated obstacles have been removed and the person is ready and at least somewhat willing to implement.
10	Regular Small-Dose Feedback and Coaching	A balanced tool for sustaining behavioral commitment. A conversation that includes honest feedback with Accountability and Respect, using the Core Dimensions to check in, provide support, remove obstacles, keep on track.	When you have identified a check-in timeframe and need a tool to help you balance your feedback; when you are planning for both proactive and reactive feedback and coaching with regards to the change and overall performance.

ADDING TO YOUR CONVERSATIONAL TOOLKIT

You've already practiced some of the key Leading Through Times of Change tools:

- Discrepancy Confrontation
- Behavior Request
- Accountability Confrontation
- Small-Dose Feedback Template

These additional tools arn't just for times of change, but are especially helpful in the midst of change.

What are some current changes in your organization or industry?

On your specific team?

With yourself personally or professionally?

Whom do you need to help navigate some of these changes?

Conversation Toolkit

	TOOL	KEY DEFINITION	WHEN TO USE
1	**Active Listening**	Listening with intent to understand the content of what is shared. Using clarifying questions and summarizing statements in conversation. Ongoing conversational tool.	When you are trying to understand the context of a situation; when you are unclear about what's going on; when the other person feels you don't understand them.
2	**Demonstrating Empathy**	Showing that you understand what someone is feeling, why they feel that way, without judgment. One of the Core Dimensions for Trust. Ongoing conversational tool.	When there is a lot of emotional content in a situation; when you need to understand how someone is feeling in order to deescalate high emotion; when the other person needs to feel heard and seen by you.
3	**Gaining Clarity**	Checking for understanding and summarizing any details, specifics, or commitments. This is about both asking and listening.	When you are asking for something specific that you want or need. When you need to make sure you have all the details you need from the other person.

Active Listening and Delivering Empathy

Notes

Video 1

The Leadership Academy: The Change Journey

Key Points

How did Sam use active listening, demonstrate empathy, and use facilitative questions?

What are the potential outcomes of using these tools in a situation like this?

Tools 1 and 2 / Active Listening and Delivering Empathy

With your Conversation Partner:

PART 1

A. Consider the important conversation you need to have with someone on your team. Take a minute or two to share with your partner some of the backstory about why you need to have this conversation.

B. Face your partner directly and make eye contact. Be fully present and remove any distractions so you can focus. Listen carefully for the content of what they are sharing. Paraphrase what you are hearing. Use phrases or clarifying questions to gain understanding.

Switch roles. When you finish, note your observations about Tool #1 Active Listening.

PART 2

A. Share more about the important conversation, this time focusing on any concerns you have about moving forward and how this might take courage or has a level or risk or uncertainty about how it will go.

B. Listen carefully for both content and feeling with regards to your partner's situation. What do you think they are feeling? Why are they feeling that way? Use an empathy statement (or two) to clarify and demonstrate that you understand. Try not to agree or disagree with them, just show that you understand what they are feeling and why about this important conversation.

Switch roles.

When you finish, note your observations about Tool #2 Demonstrating Empathy. How was this similar to or different from Tool #1. What might the impact be on a real Conversation Partner?

Notes

Video 2

The Leadership Academy: The Change Journey

Key Points

Can people really change?

When we hire someone, we want them to be able to perform well in two primary areas:

1. Technical Skills
2. Interpersonal Skills

Because it's often perceived to be easier to coach someone or give them feedback about their technical job tasks (or provide additional training), we sometimes inaccurately assess performance issues as a lack of competence or knowledge. However, we spend more time concerned with ineffective interpersonal skills that may show up as

- Negativity
- Lack of Collaboration
- Gossip
- Lack of Follow Through
- A Poor Attitude

1. How do these impact a team's performance?

Why do many leaders find it challenging to address these issues?

If you were Sam and inherited a new team member who had a reputation for being negative and difficult, what might your strategy be? Any specific Influencing Option tools that you recommend?

Video 3

The Leadership Academy: The Change Journey

Key Points

This is a confrontation between Sam and Schultz, how can you tell?

What has or has not worked when you've tried to influence someone to change their interpersonal behaviors?

GETTING UNSTUCK, SPECIAL IO TOOLS

Sometimes people can seem stuck and either unable or unwilling to move forward, whether the context is a change situation or just a need to gain momentum. You have a few Influencing Options conversational tools to help:

- Three Empowered Choices
- Behavior Request
- Personalized Deficit Question
- Accountability Confrontation

In this situation with Sam and Schultz, what should she do if he reverts to his old ways of behaving?

What is a reasonable timeframe to expect someone to change their behaviors before moving to corrective action?

REFLECTION

Considering the person whom you want to facilitate change, answer the following:

- Is the change a technical behavior?

- Is the change in interpersonal behavior?

- Which of the ten tools might be the best for where you are now in the conversation?

Notes

Share with your conversation partner.

THE CHANGE JOURNEY TEMPLATES AND GUIDES

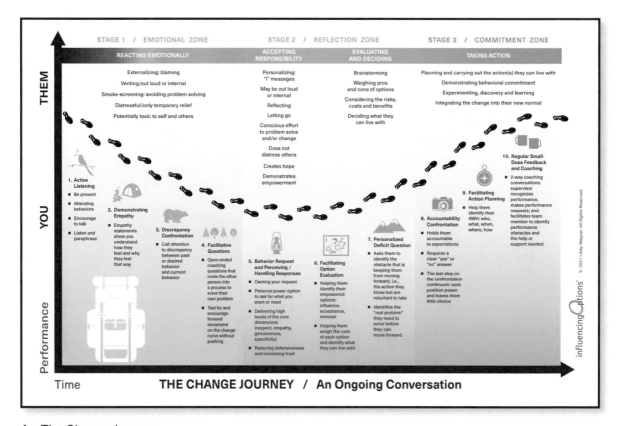

A. The Change Journey

KEY CONCEPTS

1. Individuals move through predictable stages during times of change, although rarely at the same rate.

2. Normalizing these stages helps influence movement and create trust.

3. All organizations deal with change and growth. Leaders are responsible for facilitating change using additional IO tools to help navigate change and confront when necessary.

4. Often, what we need to deal with in a change situation is someone's emotions or interpersonal behaviors.

TAKEAWAY TOOLS

Templates and Guides (See examples, left, page 50)

A.   The Change Journey

Additional conversational tools:

Active Listening

Demonstrating Empathy

Facilitative Questions

Three Empowered Choices

Personalized Deficit Action Planning

RESOURCES

1. Reading *The Influencing Option*, chapter 2.

2. Videos, *The Change Journey*, *Facilitating the Change Journey, Three Empowered Choices*

influencingOptions®

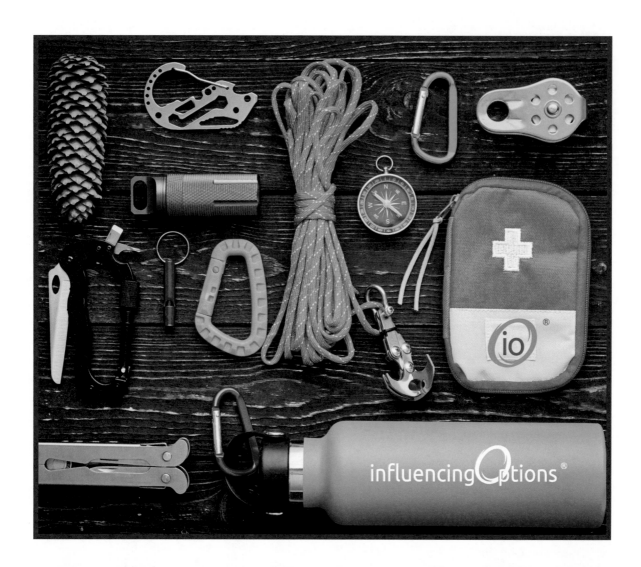

ADVANCED TOOLS

ADVANCED TOOLS FOR EFFECTIVENESS

This section may feel like a crazy hodgepodge of items, but these are practical, immediately-usable tools, templates, or hacks you can use to increase effectiveness, depending on the situation.

Tool 1: Your Team Culture

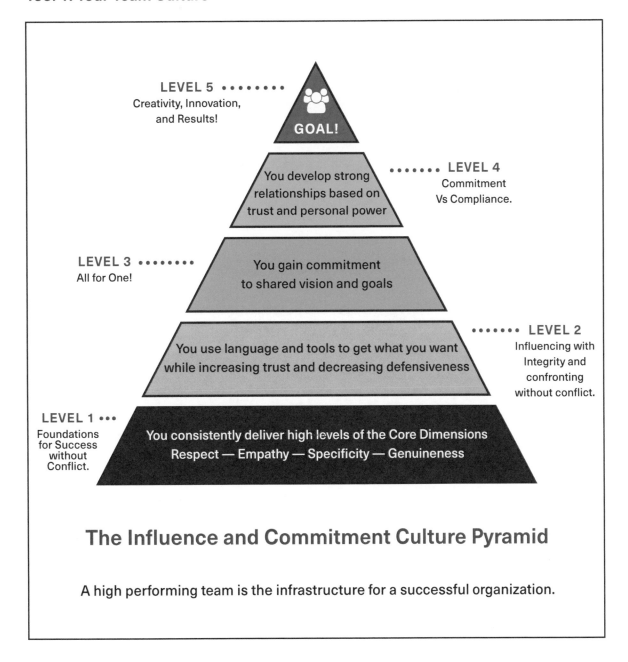

LEVEL 5 · · · · · · ·
Creativity, Innovation,
and Results!

GOAL!

You develop strong
relationships based on
trust and personal power

· · · · · · · **LEVEL 4**
Commitment
Vs Compliance.

LEVEL 3 · · · · · · · ·
All for One!

You gain commitment
to shared vision and goals

You use language and tools to get what you want
while increasing trust and decreasing defensiveness

· · · · · · · **LEVEL 2**
Influencing with
Integrity and
confronting
without conflict.

LEVEL 1 · · ·
Foundations
for Success
without
Conflict.

You consistently deliver high levels of the Core Dimensions
Respect — Empathy — Specificity — Genuineness

The Influence and Commitment Culture Pyramid

A high performing team is the infrastructure for a successful organization.

ASSESS YOUR TEAM COMMITMENT CULTURE SCALE

1. We really need some work on this.

2. We have inconsistent demonstration of strength here.

3. We have some strengths here.

4. We have consistently demonstrated strength here.

5. We are excellent at this level.

CHARACTERISTIC	YOUR SCORE (Circle 1)
1. Our team consistently delivers high levels of respect, empathy, specificity, and genuineness, and as a result, we have high trust and high resilience.	1 2 3 4 5
2. Our team is effective at influencing with integrity, internally and externally to the team, and we are good at resolving issues respectfully, quickly, and directly.	1 2 3 4 5
3. Our team has a high sense of accountability and follow through, and members see supporting one another as crucial to overall success. We are definitely on the same page.	1 2 3 4 5
4. Our team, as a rule, has consistent high performers who are models for success in the overall organization. We are more proactive than reactive and act autonomously and independently when needed.	1 2 3 4 5
5. Our team consistently meets goals/results with little fuss and distress, contributing to the overall organization's success, and rewarding creativity and innovation.	1 2 3 4 5

■ My team's strengths are:

■ My team's hotspots for improvement are:

A NOTE ABOUT POWER AND INFLUENCING

POSITION POWER	PERSONAL POWER

▪ Granted to you via the authority of your position—you're the boss!	▪ Based on the strength of your relationship and trust-building skills.
▪ Essential to use in emergency or crises where discussion and consensus may take too much time to respond.	▪ Correlates with your delivery of the Core Dimensions (respect, empathy, specificity, and genuineness) and creates an environment that supports high levels of productivity, trust, and morale.
▪ Essential to use as a last resort or the final option when you have utilized all other options to create movement, such as in improving performance.	▪ Typically makes it easier to influence the same person or group when you return for another influencing scenario.

Tool 2: Team Agreements

Never underestimate the value of a team agreement. It seems deceptively simple, but it is a powerful compass and calibrator. It both clarifies a direction and helps us get back on track. All team agreements have roots in the Core Dimensions of trust, even if they use different language.

If our team will be great AND get the results we want to fulfill the mission or vision of the organization, what would we need to be willing to do?

TEAM AGREEMENT =

Great Team AND Results, Goals, Mission or Vision Fulfilled

1. Does your team use a team agreement, guiding principles, or other types of agreement?

2. How is this an active part of team processes and conversations?

3. Does your organization have stated values (along with mission and vision)? How are those modeled and integrated into practice?

Tool 3: Four Types of Decision Making

Decisions are one of the hotspots in organizations. We want transparency. We want information. We want to know that we can be a part of decision-making. Sometimes issues arise when leaders aren't clear about what type of decision they are making and how they want others to participate.

Decisions, Decisions

Get clear about decision-making on your team, as unclear expectations and processes are a typical characteristic of Organizational Drag and can significantly impact your team's performance.

TYPE	DEFINED	WHEN
Leader	It's all about you. You decide without input or recommendation from others. You inform the team after the fact and include context, as appropriate.	In urgent or crises, or when you are responsible for the authority to make such a decision. The buck stops with you.
Leader + Input	You solicit input, data ,or opinions from the team or organization, which informs your decision. You ultimately make the decision.	When you need to gather data or information to make the best decision possible.
Leader +Recommendation	You delegate the research and gathering of data identify recommendations to the appropriate team or group. They present to you, and with your agreement, you select one of their recommendations.	When you want your team or group to be responsible for participating in the decision-making process as collaborators and to assist in creating widespread buy-in to implement the decision.
Team	You delegate not only the background work for the decision but also the decision itself. You may give parameters or guidelines, but as long as they meet expectations, you support the decision made by those you assigned.	When you want to develop your team or group and when you want to create increased autonomy and empowerment. When you want to impact your workload by positively letting go of this decision process yourself.

On your specific team, list one to two areas for decision-making that might fit into each category.

Leader

Leader + Input

Leader + Recommendation

Team

STEP	Tool 4: Standard Criteria for Decision Making	
1	Identify **the problem** first.	
2	What's **the goal** for that specific problem? (Take the problem statement and create a goal statement out of it).	
3	What are **the criteria** on which we base our decision-making?	
	A. Cost or financial impact	
	B. Ease or speed of implementation	
	C. Disruption or impact on service	
	D. Safety of clientele or staff	
	E. Risk	
	F. Political impact to organization	
	G. Meets our mission/vision (be specific)	
	H. Other	
4	Brainstorm/explore **alternatives**.	
5	**Choose an alternative** based on agreed upon criteria.	
6	Make an **action plan** with W-4.	
	Who?	
	What?	
	When?	
	Where?	
	How?	
7	**Evaluate** the outcome.	

List a team or organizational decision with multiple possible solutions that you want to resolve.

Tool 5: CAIRO Charting

CAIRO charting aims to minimize time spent on decisions or projects rather than everyone having to weigh in each time. It also provides clarification about their role and level of involvement, expected and anticipated.

SAMPLE: Issue / Topic / Project					
Person, Functional Area, Division or Group	**C**	**A**	**I**	**R**	**O**
CEO					
HR					
CFO					
Management Team					
Marketing Group					
Board Members					
IT/Technology					
Programs					
?					
?					

Take Away Tool

CAIRO Charting for Decision Making and Project Completion

C Someone (or a group) that you should CONSULT to gain input or ideas during the process or while working on a project.

A A person who has the AUTHORITY to execute decisions, i.e., the "buck stops here." This person might be the CEO, or it can also be the Board, or when appropriate, a leader should delegate this authority and responsibility.

I This is the person (group) you should INFORM of the decision that was made, i.e., memos to staff about new processes or procedures, etc.

R Who is RESPONSIBLE for actually doing the work required of the project or decision? (gathering data, research, input,etc.)

O This person (group) has NO active role in this decision or project.

Tool 6: Clearing the Swamp

Motivating—Myths & Realities

You can't motivate anyone.

- You can provide a work environment or work conditions that may be motivating to an employee.

- You can create or allow a work environment that may demotivate an employee.

- Individuals choose what motivates them.

- Different employees are motivated by different motivators.

- Different employees are de-motivated by different demotivators.

- You may have more control over influencing the demotivators by eliminating them.

- Employees are more productive when they have hope that things might improve or get better.

- Organizational de-motivators cause the majority of gossip, rumors and complaints.

Clearing the Swamp / Record and Assess

Assemble a chart of the issues or obstacles along with two other important considerations. Your chart should look something like this:

ISSUE OR OBSTACLE	CAN WE INFLUENCE IT?	IS IT WORTH IT?
1. Communication to Upper Management		
2. Budget Cuts for Equipment		
3. Getting Completed Projects from Other Teams		

Creating Action and Accountability

Creating accountability around the Clear the Swamp process involves delegating the prioritized issues the group selected and creating some action steps, timelines, and desired outcomes around them. It's essential for two reasons:

1. They identified these obstacles, agreed they could influence them and assessed their importance. That allows for ownership, so give it to them! Ensure that the team follows up —it's empowering to do so.

2. You don't need to take on the work that your team needs to be doing. Delegate, empower, back off, and check-in when appropriate.

For your team, what would be an indicator that a CTS session would be a good idea?

Tool 7: After Action Review

Journal Entry: Using an After Action Review
5 minutes writing time

First, identify a recent activity, decision, project, or occurrence that has come to an ending of some kind, i.e., completion, benchmark, etc. It might have had a positive outcome or a negative outcome.

Examining the following questions, take time to reflect, review and write down your ideas.

After Action Review (AAR) questions:

1. What were our intended results? (What was planned?)

2. What were our actual results? (What really happened?)

3. What caused our results? (Why did it happen?)

4. What will we sustain? Improve? (What can we do better next time?)

Tool 8: Meetings, Efficacy, and Effectiveness

Why are you meeting? What is the purpose?

BEST PRACTICES	WORST PRACTICES

Regular meetings

- Start and end on time.
- Clarify purpose.
- Set guidelines or intentions.
- Begin and End; set the tone.
- Share something good.
- Practice clarity and specificity.
- Mark the time 10 minutes before.
- Rotate chair, If applicable.
- Clarify notes and what happens with them.

Huddle or Stand Up Meetings

- Quick check-in.
- What's up for today? This week?
- Who needs help? Who can help?
- Celebrations or Shout-Outs.

Meeting Agenda Template

THE LEADERSHIP ACADEMY / A Conversational Approach

Meeting Agenda

Meeting Name _____   Purpose _____

Standing _____   Project _____

One-word check-in or other tone-setting element. *(Optional)* _____

1. Good news and gratitudes: _____

_____

2. Agenda items/topics, including: intentions, discussions, decisions, or actions.

1. _____   4. _____

2. _____   5. _____

3. _____   6. _____

3. Any potential bottlenecks or issues we haven't discussed. _____

_____

4. About 10 minutes until the end, pause and clarify:

Next Steps Actions: *Who:*

1. _____   1. _____

2. _____   2. _____

3. _____   3. _____

Share takeaways or offer a closing. *(Optional)* _____

5. End on time.

Meeting Assesment Tool

1.   List all meetings currently on your schedule that you attend and/or run.
2.   Assess meetings and identify any changes or recommendations.

	Meeting	Meeting	Meeting	Meeting
Meeting (Name, Date, etc.)				
Purpose Goal or Outcome				
Standing or Project Focused?				
Who attends?				
How is the time used?				
Is there an agenda? Minutes?				
Suggested changes and/or recommendations?				

Tool 9: Recognition Basics

If they're doing their job, performing to standard, isn't their pay or salary enough?

No! Recognition is a powerful performance management tool, in addition to being the "right" thing to do with your employees.

Types of Recognition:

1. Consistent performance

2. Above-and-beyond performance

3. Career milestones or benchmarks

List the current formal or informal ways you recognize or reward performance in your workplace or on your team?

Elements for Recognition:

1. Be sincere.

2. Be specific.

3. Tell why it's important.

4. Do it now.

10

Small-Dose Feedback Conversation Template
A Balanced Approach

SUPERVISOR

1. Recognition of accomplishment or positive reinforcement of genuine attempt(s)

"I _____

How you feel about what they've done.

_____

specifically, the way you _____

_____

Specific behaviors you are recognizing/reinforcing.

and as a result, _____

_____

Positive impact of their behaviors.

_____."

Who do I need to recognize this week?

Tool 10: Making Presentations, Giving Talks, and Speaking in Public

As a leader, you will often need to speak on behalf of your team, program, or organization. List common opportunities for you to speak in the space below.

Outline	Template for Planning a Speech or Presentation
I. Beginning	**Start powerfully. Share a story, an interesting statistic, a piece of data, or pose a provocative question.** ■ You might indicate the purpose or intention of your talk. ■ You might share a brief outline.
	Transition statement.
II. Body of Talk	**Organize your thoughts and create a logical progression.** ■ Make your key points. ■ Provide examples, models, or stories to illustrate.
	Transition statement.
III. Q & A	**If you include a Q&A portion, put it BEFORE your closing.** ■ Answer briefly, if possible, or promise to follow up. ■ Pay attention to your time.
	Transition statement.
IV: Closing	**End powerfully.** ■ You may want to summarize. ■ Present a call to action, an invitation, or next steps. ■ Include a thank you statement. ■ Consider your very last statement or words. How are you leaving?

Other Speaking Tips:

■ Appeal to both logic and emotion, especially if you want people to do something.
■ Practice: prepare key points.
■ Don't read your speech.
■ Don't PowerPoint people to death; a few images are more powerful (or none!)
■ If you plan to be interactive, you might share guiding principles for doing so.
■ Know your strengths and challenges and be willing to improve.

FINAL THOUGHTS

Pick two of the advanced tools. You will use in the next month and share your plan.

Advanced Tools for Effectiveness

Tool 1: Your Team Culture

Tool 2: Team Agreements

Tool 3: Four Types of Decision Making

Tool 4: Standard Criteria for Decision Making

Tool 5: CAIRO Charting

Tool 6: Clearing the Swamp

Tool 7: After Action Review

Tool 8: Meetings, Efficacy, and Effectiveness

Tool 9: Recognition Basics

Tool 10: Making Presentations, Giving Talks, and Speaking in Public

Tool number _____
My Plan:

Tool number _____
My Plan:

KEY CONCEPTS

Use these practical tools to increase efficiency and effectiveness.

1. Prepare and be proactive by beginning with the end in mind.

2. Use meetings, projects, and conversations as ways to both get things done and build team trust.

3. Use the Template for Planning a Speech or Presentation to draft an outline for your talk.

TAKEAWAY TOOLS

Templates and Guides

A. The Influence and Commitment Culture Pyramid

B. The Team Agreement

C. Standard Criteria for Decision Making

D. CAIRO Charting

E. Accountability Chart

F. Meeting Agenda Template

G. Meeting Assesment Tool

H. Template for Planning a Speech or Presentation

RESOURCES

1   Read *The Influencing Option*, chapters 5, 8, 9.

2.   Influencing Options Video: *Three Empowered Choices.*

C. Standard Criteria for Decision Making

F. Meeting Agenda Template

G. Meeting Assesment Tool

H. Template for Planning a Speech or Presentation

influencing Options®

Your 90,000 Hours : Wholeheartedness at Work

RIGHT RELATIONSHIP TO LIVELIHOOD

What leaders really need is a right relationship to their livelihood: to have harmony and joy, to have a sense of satisfaction and celebration, to experience real relationships and create a powerful impact.

90,000 hours is a lot of time to invest in one's livelihood and deserves thoughtful, purposeful consideration and meaningful action. As always, we begin with you.

Most leaders want to do good work, lead with courage, and have lives that are connected to the people, places, and things they value. And yet, burnout, overwhelm, and high stress are often consequences of the leadership path. Is this inevitable? If you say 'yes' to leading, does that mean you say 'no' to a whole life that's fulfilling?

Define right relationship to livelihood for you.

influencingOptions®

DEFINING YOUR WHOLEHEARTEDNESS

Wholeheartedness at work is a daily practice; it's not something you get from reading a book, listening to a podatus or even attending a workshop. The goal of this section is to create a chance for reflection, robust discussion and connection to that which is important.

The pressure is always for more, faster, better—not necessarily negative pursuits in themselves, but at what cost to individuals, teams, or communities?

> It is difficult
> to get the news from poems
> yet men die miserably every day
> for lack
> of what is found there.
>
> — William Carlos Williams

Element 1
Reflecting and Self-Assessment

Developing self-awareness is one gift of being fully human. Any wholehearted journey must begin with understanding who you are, what's important to you, what brings you joy so that you can know when you are in or out of integrity, when you are congruent and when you are not. Exhaustion and burnout at work happen when we are not harmonious and not aligned with ourselves. Feeling stuck means, we may feel like we are not spending time on things that matter to us. When we recognize when we are in the "flow," "in the groove," or in our "sweet spot" with work, we can also tell when we are not. Reflecting and assessing is a helpful way to recalibrate and get honest with ourselves about what matters.

Share insights about your journal pre-work in your breakout groups.

Best Practices for Reflection and Self-Assessment

CURRENT	TO PRACTICE

Element 2
Letting Go

Part of the natural course of human evolution is to begin again or begin anew. There are many opportunities in a lifetime to reinvent or reinvigorate. We are called to this renewal repeatedly, but only if we are willing to let go of the place we currently inhabit. We have innate, intuitive wisdom that lets us know when it is time to move toward that threshold of the future, of the horizon, coupled with the knowledge that, indeed, we must give up that which is the current state of our perceived reality. If we pay attention, we are arrested by this knowing; that it is time to move on—feelings of exhaustion, impatience, boredom, and some levels of despair can be indicators of divine discontent. It is an opportunity to recognize that it is time to let go of the old story we've been telling ourselves, the old conversation that has worn thin of any element of surprise or wonder. At its core, stopping the conversation is an emergence of a new sort of truth. We know this on a deep level, and we also know it is the coexistence of both loss and light. As leaders, it's easy to become trapped in the same conversations, the same stories about what makes our businesses and organizations the way they are. We eventually develop belief patterns over time that no longer serve us. We become tired of the

political push and pull the hidden agendas, the not talking about what's important. In our roles as conversational leaders, we are called to heighten our awareness and be willing to notice when these indicators of divine discontent show up not only within ourselves but also among our colleagues, with our stakeholders, and customers. We know that to create, innovate, and fulfill the mission of our work, we must regularly be ready "to abandon the shoes that brought [us] here," to find a new path by letting go of a portion of the history we've created together.

List three to five things that are just not working for you right now.... can you let them go? If not, why? What if you don't?

Element 3
Walkabouts: More on the Art of Noticing

Over thirty years ago, Ken Blanchard made famous his "managing by walking around" philosophy in the book The One-Minute Manager. It's still a good philosophy; to be out and about, amongst the employees, close to the work, and the customer experience. In recent years, the Emmy Award-winning reality TV show, *Undercover Boss*, created opportunities for corporate bosses, far from the front lines of their businesses, to see what it was like to work in the lowest levels of jobs in their organizations.

Regardless of the size of your organization—even if you are only occasionally out and about—your walkabouts should include the art and practice of noticing. Noticing (aka paying attention) is what poets do because we turn up our awareness to try to make some sense of our world, our relationships, or the human experience. And, since we are taking care and taking time, we are often the ones who can find just the right words at the right time to say the unsayable.

However, the art and practice of noticing at work is troublesome because it's counterintuitive to the ordinary pace of contemporary organizational life. We run from meeting to meeting, conference calls, and double-booked calendars. We eat at our desks (if at all), and now we have to stand up desks or treadmill desks so we can pretend to be doing all sorts of things while answering our emails. We rush and cram and worry, none of which helps at all with noticing. If it's seemingly impossible, why even talk about it?

There are costs and benefits related to noticing, all of which directly impact your organization's success, your employee's engagement, your client's loyalty, and your satisfaction and joy. Noticing has big payoffs and dire consequences if neglected. Most leaders cannot just decide one day to be better at this—our busy habits are well engrained. I recommend doing some "research" to see how you might increase your practice. Just like most of us could not just go out tomorrow and run a marathon without some training or practice, improving your noticing quotient needs that sort of attention and commitment, too.

Where do you need to take more notice? What would that look like? What do you need?

Some ideas for practice

1. **In your to-work transition:** Do you have a commute? A car or train ride? A walk or bike route to work? If so, how can you practice noticing while on this important transition to your workday? Many of us listen to the radio, music, or even schedule calls during this time. Experiment and pick at least two days a week where you have nothing other than the actual movement from place to place. No radio, podcasts, or calls.Maybe even no conversation. What do you notice, both internally and externally? How are you feeling? What's your mood or sense of anticipation for the day? What do you sense (see, hear, etc.) on the actual journey?

2. **Select one person/meeting/interaction per day** and become utterly present to it. Do not multitask. Focus entirely on what's at hand, or the person in front of you, or on the phone. Decide to listen carefully and perhaps demonstrate empathy. What do you notice? Are you anxious? Excited? Annoyed? Is there an opportunity for a Beautiful (provocative and expansive) Question or opening? Is there a space for creativity or innovation from an idea or concept that you notice?

3. **Examine your calendar, diary, or schedule** to see if you have any spaciousness or whether you are booked solid, back-to-back every day this week? Do you have time allotted for lunch or an afternoon stretch walk? Is there a place you can block out 30 minutes you call sacred to take time to notice what has happened before this time and what's to come following? Noticing, ultimately, is about presence and being in the moment. It's hard to do this when there are no transitions built-in.

4. **Create a from-work transition.** There's been quite a bit of research in the past few years on the impact of gratitude on the quality of work and the happiness quotient.

5. **10 Things Practice: Noticing muscles need a workout.** Take 5 to 10 minutes and get outside if possible. Jot down ten specific descriptive statements about what you notice. Try not to use metaphor or simile, just pure description using your senses.

 See Martin Seligman's work www.pursuit-of-happiness.org.

Reflect on the day. What did you notice? For what are you grateful? Where are you glad for a "do-over" for tomorrow?

Element 4
Creating Spaciousness

Most of us cram too many things into our calendars; it's not even that we don't have buffers. We are often double or triple booked. Where can you begin to create more spaciousness? Begin with your intentions, then start where you are now.

Step 1
Create a Baseline Practice

Baseline is a concept from productivity expert Leah Fisch.
What are the five to eight things you need to do, so you can do what you need to do? How can you set yourself up to 'win'?

1. —————————————————————————————————————

2. —————————————————————————————————————

3. —————————————————————————————————————

4. —————————————————————————————————————

5. —————————————————————————————————————

6. —————————————————————————————————————

7. —————————————————————————————————————

8. —————————————————————————————————————

Step 2
Your Ideal Schedule

Create an ideal schedule with blocks of time for meetings, breaks, reflection, and the other things you want to do. Include the weekend. Use colors if you wish.

TIME/PERIOD	MONDAY	TUESDAY	WEDNESDAY	THURSDAY	FRIDAY

Weekend Intentions:

How far away are you from this ideal schedule? What's one thing you could change now?

Step 3
Assess your workload

Look at your current calendar as it is. List as many meetings, projects, programs, or functions over which you have responsibility. Take time to rank and assess.

Leadership Workload Assessment

Ranking:
A.   I'm the final authority; pertinent regulatory requirements; no one else can do this.
B.   I have special talents here; I model the standard for excellence; I'm responsible for the big picture (I like doing this).
C.   Has to get done; could be delegated, shared, or create a development opportunity.

Rank	Task, Function, or Meeting	What's Uniquely Mine to do?	Who are my supporters, collaborators or people?	Opportunities for delegation or development?

Examine your assessment for delegation opportunities. Refer to Delegation Diagnostic in *The Influencing Options,* chapter 9.

What are two actions you can take immediately to impact your workload?

1. _____

2. _____

Element 5
What is Radical Self-Care? A Radical Approach to Dealing with Change

Most of us are busy. Scheduled. Booked and triple-booked. Many people will sacrifice things they see as non-essential as they worship at the church of busyness: your sleep, your nutrition, your exercise, your time with others, even your time with yourself. Even though we talk about "work-life balance," and we desire it, we crave it. It's a myth. We don't balance anything because our days are forever unpredictable and changing themselves. What we need to be able to do is to show up in our conversations and interactions with the presence and focus that tumultuous times demand. If we are sleep deprived, emotionally exhausted, or detached from those we love, we have very little from which to draw upon to manage the stressors that consistent change brings.

If this is not a current practice of yours, then it's likely bringing up two primary responses: **the logistics** of it: i.e., how can you possibly make time for self-care when you don't have time to deal with your outrageous to-do list? And, **the desire** for it: Could I really go to bed earlier? Could I really schedule a massage or go for a walk on a summer evening? Could I really have an agenda-less hour?

Nike already captured the best advice with regards to the above: ***JUST DO IT!*** But it's more than that. You often have to give yourself permission for radical self-care. And, it's radical because it doesn't make sense. It's radical because no one else is doing it. It's radical because many of us have bought into the idea that we don't deserve it or that we are unworthy of it. If that doesn't resonate with you, I invite you to check your relationship with perfectionism 1—that's just worthiness in disguise.

Right now, what would feel radical (out of the ordinary, a little risky) to you regarding your self-care?

Here are some suggestions to consider, but make your own list. Only you know your edges for radicalism when it comes to self-care!

- <u>Schedule a massage, acupuncture, or other health treatment</u> for your body. We forget that our bodies hold us, carry us, and sustain us, especially when we are busy.

- <u>Schedule a walk (or movement) in a place you love</u>, like a park, garden, beach, or street. Even if it's just 30 minutes, engage your senses by being present on the walk: don't talk on the phone or even listen to music, if you can do it!

- <u>Manage your intake of news, social media, and information.</u> This is tough for many, but even if you can do an experiment for a week, shift your focus and say "yes" to yourself rather than "yes" to the world at large. This is about rejuvenating your spirit.

- <u>Acknowledge your feelings, especially grief and loss.</u> We experience this range of emotions, from the slightest disappointment to the grandest trauma. Unexpressed grief and loss are the painful foundation for illness, stress, and many other psychological ailments. Have a trusted confidant? Talk or share. Work with a therapist? Get the support you need.

- <u>Reframe when possible.</u> Seeing challenges as opportunities doesn't mean you take a spiritual by-pass of what's happening (see the above point). Still, it does mean that you can begin to reframe how you might deal with a stressful or unavoidable situation at work or home.

- <u>Hold the vision for yourself and others.</u> Keep the end in mind. Whether it's a project, a company, a program, stay connected to the ideal vision of it, remind yourself why and what's the purpose of what you are doing. Connecting with purpose is life-sustaining.

- <u>Spend time with people who matter to you.</u> Every artistic tradition in every culture reminds us to focus on what matters, and what matters is love. Everything else pales in comparison. Whether it's beloved friends, a partner or spouse, a child, a pet, we are not meant to be solitary characters floating in time and space.

In an *On Being* interview with Krista Tippett and poet Marie Howe, they talked about poetry and things that matter to them. When Marie Howe asked the question, "Which face is the one I gaze into the most?" we all held our collective breaths, because we all knew it was the smartphone, or some other screen, the things that tie us to our busy-ness, not to the ones we love. Maybe the smallest, most radical act might be just that: to gaze into another's face more often.

How can you plan a screenless time with someone special?

Element 6
Engaging in Courageous Conversations

This conversation is the conversation you don't want to have, but you know you need to have it. If we stop in the space created by letting go of the old conversation and sitting with the beautiful question, we emerge the wisdom and understanding of the conversation that needs to happen next. This may be a conversation with self, with others, with the larger world. It is a conversation that requires a certain kind of confidence, connected to the root of the word: con (with) +fidere (faith). Not the boastful, arrogant cousin of confidence, but the bold, courageous confidence of trusting the unknown and moving forward, taking action in this conversation anyway, in the face of risk, despite the risk, because you know you can not, not have the conversation.

In organizations, there is a rampant lack of courageous conversations. The ICL outline of the Five Courageous Conversations is a place to begin, a series of questions about whether or not the kinds of conversations that need to be had are actually flourishing. It is the leader's job to instigate these conversations at every level, and it takes courage, confidence, trust, faith, risk. This may be one of the most challenging aspects of leadership, fostering both an environment and a methodology for the courageous conversation and being brave enough to both invite it and listen.

Five Essential Courageous Conversations for Organizational Leaders

5. What is the courageous conversation we are not yet having with the unknown future —the world that lies over the horizon but has not yet been fully articulated?

4. What is the courageous conversation we are not yet having with our clients or the society (industry/science/?) of which we are a part? This, in effect, is the future now, the currents of people and events that flow around the organization and the endeavors of the individuals who make it up?

3. What is the courageous conversation we are not yet having between the divisions and cultures within the organization? What prevents us from taking another step in working together?

2. What is the courageous conversation I am not yet having in my immediate work-group or with my direct supervisors, associates, or subordinates? What is the courageous conversation I can personally initiate to start things moving in this close circle?

1. What is the conversation I am refusing to have with myself, in my own heart and mind about my work and the present life threshold on which I find myself? What is the courageous conversation I am not yet having with my partner or spouse, children, or loved ones?

You have the tools! Which of these feel the most important to you right now? Where can you show up with your voice more courageously?

Element 7
Cultivating Relationships and Support

Even though most organizations and teams desire collaboration, cooperation, and interdependence, the higher you go in your leadership journey, the more likely you will feel isolated and alone.

Who are the people who support you both professionally and personally.? Where do you find guidance, solace, truth, empathy, or other things you need?

At Work?

Personal Relationships and Friendships?

Professional Services?

Which person would be great to reach out to now? When can you do that?
Bonus, put it on your calendar!

Element 8
Taking Time

No one reaches the end of their lives and says, "Wow, I wish I would have worked more!" It's a cliché, but that doesn't mean it's not true.

Often we create artificial "somedays" with regards to the way we spend our time.

What's on your Someday List?

Someday I'd like to . . . .(do, be, see . . .)

What are you waiting for? Could you begin now or sooner than someday?

List three things that might need to happen next to get you closer.

KEY CONCEPTS

1. Managing your own workload takes discipline, practice and delegating.
2. You're responsible for your engagement and peace of mind.
3. Radical self-care is usually the answer.
4. Set yourself up to "win."

TAKEAWAY TOOLS

Templates and Guides

A. Weekly Planner Template
B. Leadership Workload Assessment
C. Delegation Diagnostic
D. Takeaway Practices

RESOURCES

1. Reading *The Influencing Option*, chapters 9 and 10.

2. *What Will You Do With Your 90,000 Hours?* e-book.

A. Weekly Planner Template

B. Leadership Workload Assessment

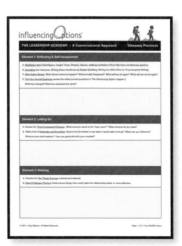

D. Takeaway Practices